AMERICAN Chatterbox

STUDENT BOOK
Starter

DEREK STRANGE

OXFORD UNIVERSITY PRESS

Oxford University Press
198 Madison Avenue
New York, NY 10016 USA

Walton Street
Oxford OX2 6DP England

OXFORD is a trademark of Oxford University Press.

Copyright © 1996 Oxford University Press

Library of Congress Cataloging-in-Publication Data

Strange, Derek.
    American chatterbox starter. Student book / Derek Strange.
       p. cm. — (Oxford American English)
      ISBN 0-19-434564-5 (student bk.). — ISBN 0-19434584-X (teacher's book.). — ISBN 0-19-434585-8 (workbk.). — ISBN 0-19-434586-6 (cassette)
    1. English language—Textbooks for foreign speakers—Juvenile literature. [1. English language—Textbooks for foreign speakers.]
I. Title. II. Series.
PE1128.S865 1995
428.2'4—dc20   94-39158

No unauthorized photocopying

All rights reserved. No part of this publication may be reproduced, stored in a retrieval system, or transmitted, in any form or by any means, electronic, mechanical, photocopying, recording, or otherwise, without the prior written permission of Oxford University Press.

This book is sold subject to the condition that it shall not, by way of trade or otherwise, be lent, resold, hired out, or otherwise circulated without the publisher's prior consent in any form of binding or cover other than that in which it is published and without a similar condition being imposed on the subsequent purchaser.

Printing (last digit): 10 9 8 7 6 5 4 3 2

Printed in Hong Kong.

Strange, Derek
    American chatter box starter: student book/
Derek Strange.— Esfahan: Jangal, 1378 = 2000.
    62 p.: illus. col.
    Reprint of 1996ed., Oxford University Press,
    ISBN 0-19-434564-5.
    Cataloging based on CIP information.
    Publisher varies in different editions.

    1.English language - Textbooks for foreign speakers - Juvenile literature. I.Title.

PE1128.A2S76   428.24
1996a
National lib. of Iran   M78-24486

شناسنامه کتاب

نام کتاب: American Chatter box starter (Student book)

نویسنده: Derek Strang

تاریخ و نوبت چاپ: دهم ۱۳۸۶

تیراژ: ۱۰۰۰۰ جلد

چاپ و صحافی:

ناشر: انتشارات جنگل

تلفن: 66921166-66924542-021

0311-2212047-2239809

Unit 1

Hello!

1 Listen.

2 Listen and say.

Say hello.

Annie Shep Lucy Herman

Unit 1

📼 Look!

Unit 1

Stop!

4 Listen and match.

Play a game: Simon says…

1. Simon says: Come here.

2. Simon says: Come here, please.

OK.

4 Unit 1

a b c

5 **Sing.**

Unit 2

Hi! I'm Lucy.

6 Listen and match.

Wait! Goodbye! Hi! I'm Lucy. Goodbye!

Goodbye! Hi! I'm Annie. Hello! I'm Herman.

Unit 2

I'm Zoko.

Unit 2

What's this?

Look and say.

a girl   a boy   a box   a robot   a bicycle

⏵8 Listen and match.

Ask and answer.

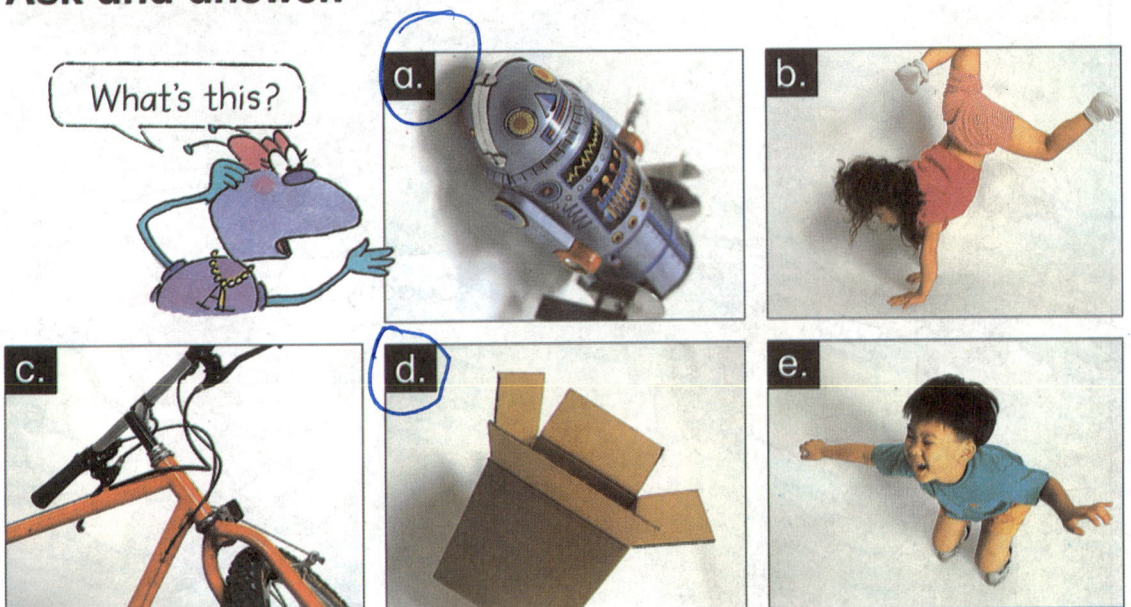

What's this?

a.
b.
c.
d.
e.

Unit 2

🎵 Hello! Goodbye!

9 Sing.

Hello! Hello! Hello!
Hi! Hi! Hi!
Sing! Sing! Sing!
Goodbye! Goodbye! Goodbye!
G o o d b y e !
G o o d b y e !
G o o d b y e !

Goodbye!

Unit 3

What's this?

Look.

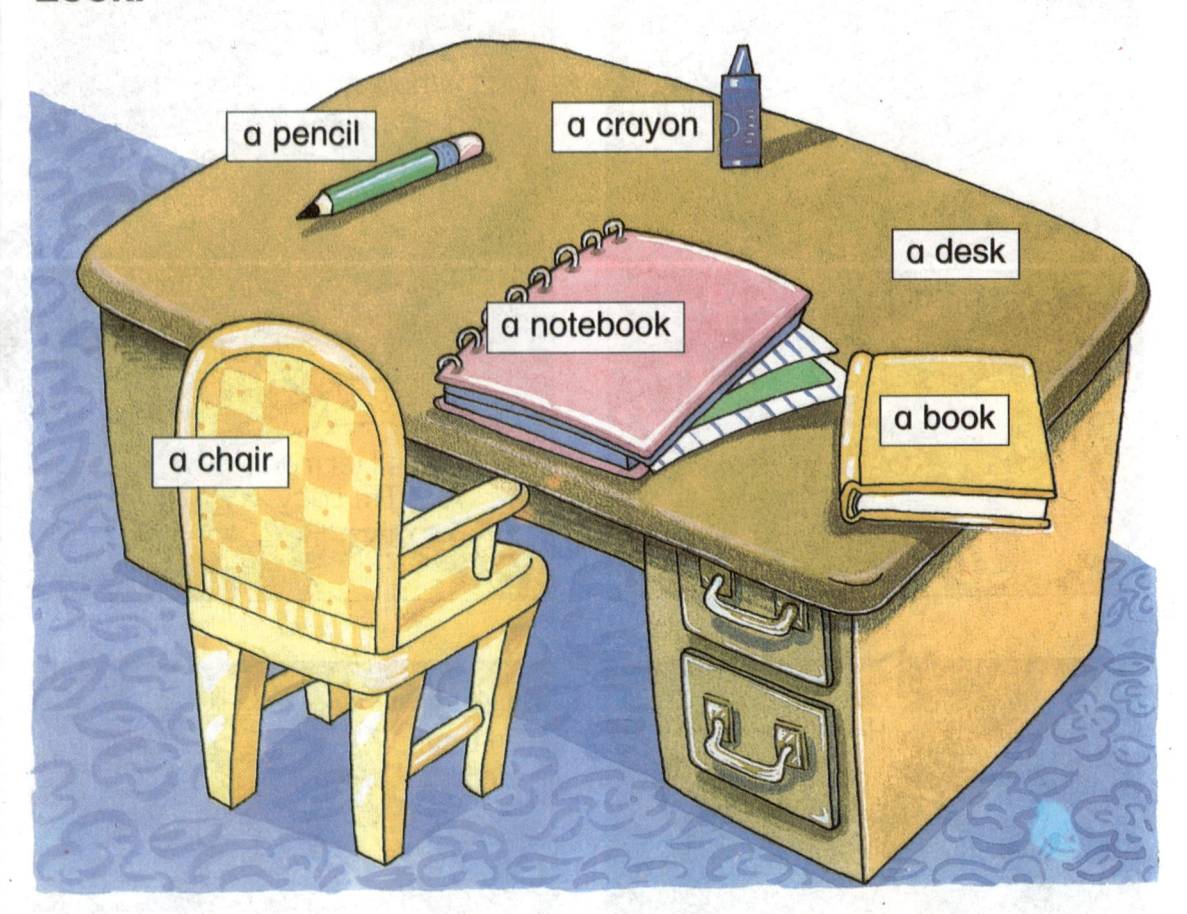

- a pencil
- a crayon
- a desk
- a notebook
- a book
- a chair

10 Listen.

Give me a..., please.

Thank you.

Unit 3

Who's this?

1. What's this? — A robot.
2. Who's this? — This is Herman. And I'm Lucy.
3. Hello, Lucy. Hello, Herman. I'm Zoko. — Hello, Zoko.
4. Lucy! Herman! Listen! Who's this?

Unit 3

Who's this?

Look and say: *This is...*

12 Listen.

"Who's this?"

Unit 3

♪ Who's This?

🎧 ¹³ **Sing.**

Who's this? Who's this?
Who's this?

Who's this? Who's this?
Who's this?

Who's this? Who's this?
Who's this?

Unit 4

My name?

📼 ¹⁴ Listen.

What's your name?

My name? My name's Antonia.

ZOKO

📼 ¹⁵ Listen and repeat.

Aa Bb Cc Dd Ee Ff Gg Hh Ii
Jj Kk Ll Mm Nn Oo Pp Qq
Rr Ss Tt Uu Vv Ww Xx Yy Zz

Play a game: How do you spell...?

How do you spell my name?

A...N...T...

Unit 4

What's your name?

1. This is my brother.
2. What's your name? — My name's Shep. Lucy is my sister.
3. What's your name? — My name's Zoko.
4. Hello, Shep. — Hi, Zoko.

Unit 4

My brother, my sister, and my friend

🔊¹⁷ Listen.

What's your name?

My name's Antony.

This is my brother.

My name's Ann.

This is my sister.

This is my friend.

My name's Andy.

🔊¹⁷ Listen again.

Anson   Angela   Andrea   Anita   André

16　　　　　　　　　　　　　　　　　　　　　　　Unit 4

♪ How Are You?

🎵¹⁸ Sing.

My name's Kenny.
My name's Kenny.

My name's Sue.
My name's Sue.

Hi! What's your name?
Hi! What's your name?
How are you?
How are you?

I'm fine, thank you.

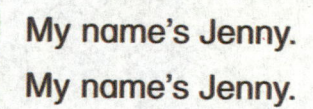

My name's Jenny.
My name's Jenny.

My name's Lou.
My name's Lou.

Hi! What's your name?
Hi! What's your name?
How are you?
How are you?

Unit 5

17

An octopus, an insect, and an egg

Look.

- an umbrella
- an octopus
- an insect
- an egg
- an ant

Look! It's an octopus!

▣ ¹⁹ **Listen.**

Point to an octopus.

Unit 5

It's a bicycle.

1. What's this? — It's a bicycle.
2. It's my bicycle. — Yes. A bicycle. It's your bicycle.
3. Hello, Bicycle. I'm Zoko. — No, Zoko!
4. Oh, great! Listen!

Unit 5

19

Look again.

Listen.

What's this?
It's a...

Play a game.

a...b...c...d...
Stop!
It's a desk.
Yes!

Unit 5

🎵 The Bicycle Song

Sing.

It's a bi- bi- bi- bi- bicycle!
It's a bicycle! It's a bicycle!
It's a bi- bi- bi- bi- bicycle!
It's a bi- bi- bicycle!

It's a ro- ro- ro- ro- robot!
It's a robot! It's a robot!
It's a ro- ro- ro- ro- robot!
It's a ro- ro- robot!

It's a robot! It's a bicycle!
It's a robot and a bike!
It's a robot and a bicycle!
It's a robot and a bike!

Unit 6

Balloons!

📼²³ Listen and look.

1 one
2 two
3 three
4 four
5 five
6 six
7 seven
8 eight
9 nine
10 ten

📼²⁴ Listen. Count with Zoko.

21

Unit 6

📼 It's an elevator.

1. Look! It's an elevator.
Come on, Bicycle. It's an elevator.

2. HELP!
No, Zoko! Stop!
Oh, Zoko!

| 1 | 2 | 3 | 4 | 5 | 6 | 7 | 8 | 9 | 10 |

3. Stop, Elevator! Please stop!

4. Hello! Who are you?
Hello. I'm Zoko.

Unit 6

23

How old are you?

🔊 26 Listen and match.

How old are you?

🔊 27 Listen

Hi! How old are you?

I'm six.

And we're seven.

I don't know.

Number Samba

🔊²⁸ Sing and dance.

One…two…
One…two…three…
One…two…three…four…five.

One…two…
One…two…three…
One…two…three…four…five.

Six…seven…
Six…seven…eight…
Six…seven…eight…nine…ten.

Six…seven…
Six…seven…eight…
Six…seven…eight…nine…ten.

Unit 6

Unit 7

25

She's six, he's eight.

▶️²⁹ **Listen and look.**

▶️³⁰ **Now listen and match.**

Draw a badge.

Play a game: How old...?

1. With your badge
2. With no badge

Unit 7

I'm a clown.

1.
— Hello, Zoko. How are you?
— I'm Montgomery. I'm a clown.

2.
— She's ten. He's nine. He's eight, and she's seven.
— They're twins— they're six.
— Yes! We're six. We're twins.

3.
— She's ten. He's nine. He's eight, and she's seven. And they're six. OK.
— And how old are you, Zoko?

4.
— I don't know.
— Be quiet! Listen! Who's this?

Unit 7

27

It's her hat; they're his shoes.

📼 32 **Listen.**

Look and say: *His balloon* or *Her balloon*.

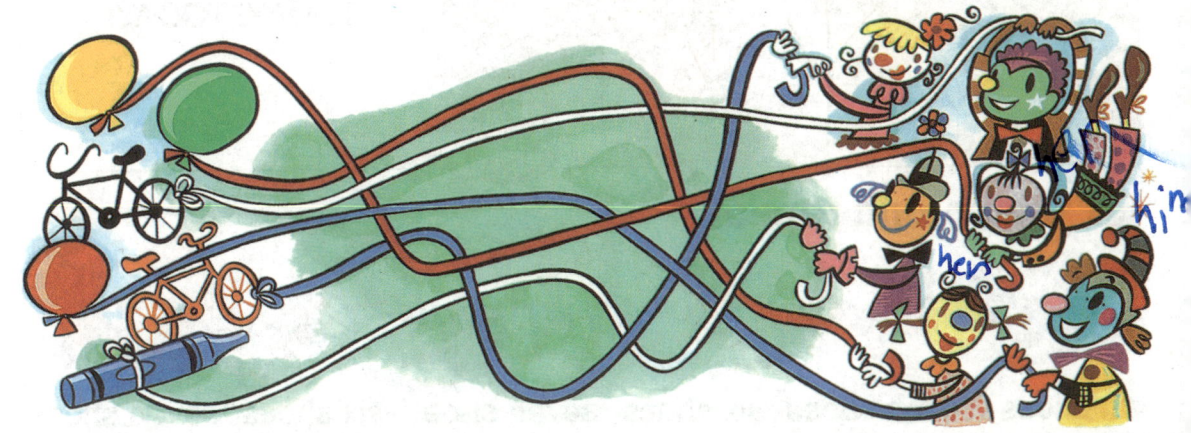

Unit 7

♪ Today! Today!

🎵³³ Sing.

I'm a clown,
I'm a clown,
And my circus
Is in town...
TODAY! TODAY!

He's a clown,
He's a clown,
And his circus
Is in town...
TODAY! TODAY!

I'm a clown,
I'm a clown,
And my circus
Is in town...
TODAY! TODAY!

She's a clown,
She's a clown,
And her circus
Is in town...
TODAY! TODAY!

🎵³⁴ Listen and repeat.

six shoes   seven shoes   six shoes   seven shoes   six shoes   seven shoes

Unit 8

29

Is it an airplane?

🎧³⁵ Listen and match.

- a car
- an airplane
- a truck
- a robot
- a bike
- a clown

"Is it an airplane?"
"Is it a truck?"
"No, it isn't."
"Yes, it is! It's a truck!"

Look.

| Is it a bike? | Yes, it is! | No, it isn't. |

A. B. C. D. E. F. G.

Unit 8

Is it a monster?

1. Be quiet! Listen! Who's this? — WHOOOOAAAAAAAAAAAAAAA — Is it a ghost?

2. Ha! Ha! No, it isn't! — Is it a police car?

3. No! No, it isn't! It isn't a police car! Ha! Ha! Ha! — EEEEEEEEEE — Is it a monster?

4. A monster? Ha! Ha! Yes, it is! It's Lucy! She's my friend.

Unit 8

Big or small?

🔊 37 Listen and match.

1. Here's a big crayon.
2. Here's a big ice cream cone.
3. Here's a big cookie. *small*
4. Great! A big bubble.

Now read and match.

- It isn't a big bubble. It's a small bubble.
- It isn't a big crayon. It's small.
- It isn't big. It's a small ice cream cone.
- It isn't a big cookie. It's a small cookie.

Play a game: What's this?

What's this? It's a _box_.

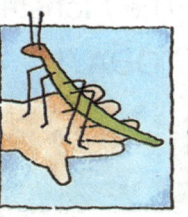

Unit 8

🎵 The Monster Ball

Sing.

Hello, monsters,
Big and small!
Come and dance
At the Monster Ball.

The Monster Ball. The Monster Ball.
The Monster Ball. OK?
The Monster Ball. The Monster Ball.
The Monster Ball. TODAY!

Unit 9

The blue balloon

🎧39 Listen and match.

brown
blue
yellow
green
black
red
orange
white

Look! Here are the balloons again.

The blue balloon is number two.

The blue balloon
Is number two,
Number two, number two.
The blue balloon
Is number two.
Blue! Blue! Blue!

🎧40 Listen and repeat.

🎧41 Listen and repeat.

blue balloon
yellow balloon
blue balloon
yellow balloon
blue balloon
yellow balloon

Unit 9

At the circus

1. We're from the circus. — The circus?

2. Yes. The Red, White, and Blue Circus. Look! — They're from the circus! Great!

3. Come and see Simba the Lion. He's from Africa. — And this is Dana the Elephant. She's from India.

4. And this is Mr. Stink. He's the boss. — Yes, I'm the boss. I'm from England. And who are you?

Unit 9

35

The color wheel

Make a color wheel.

1. Draw the wheel.
2. Cut the wheel.
3. Color the wheel.

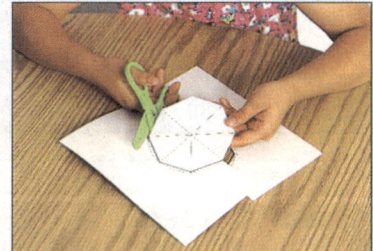

This is the color wheel.

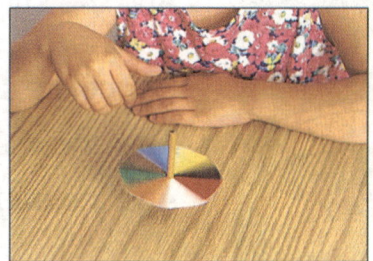

Now play a game with the wheel.

Spin the wheel. Say a color.

Yellow, please.

Red, please.

Blue, please.

What color is it?

It's yellow!

The Sun Is Yellow.

Sing.

Grass is green,
The sky is blue,
And the sun is yellow!

Chocolate's brown,
And snow is white,
And the sun is yellow!

Snow is white,
And grass is green,
And the sun is yellow!

The sky is blue,
And chocolate's brown,
And the sun is yellow!

Unit 10

Faces

🔊 Listen and repeat.

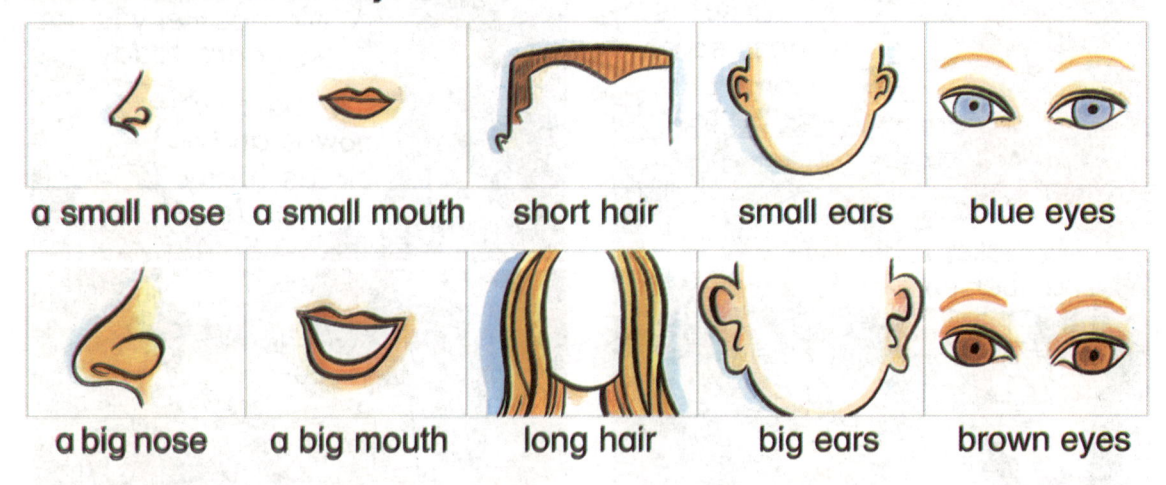

| a small nose | a small mouth | short hair | small ears | blue eyes |
| a big nose | a big mouth | long hair | big ears | brown eyes |

🔊 Listen and match.

"I have a red nose."

Choose a face. Play a game: Who's this?

"Listen. Who's this? She has orange hair. She has a green nose."

Unit 10

🔊 He has a big, red nose.

1. My ticket is number six.

   My ticket is number seven. Come on!

2. Be quiet, please! I'm sorry, but Montgomery is not here today.

   We have no clowns and no circus today, friends.

   What? No clowns?

3. Montgomery is our friend. He has a big, red nose. He has a white mouth.

   And he has short hair. His hair is yellow.

4. He's tall and thin. He has long legs and long arms.

   Lucy, look! It's a number!

   HELP! 946-8753

Unit 10

39

Look again.

🔊⁴⁷ Listen and point.

	A	B	C	D
1	car	elephant	monster	balloon
2	lion	bicycle	car	airplane
3	mouse	airplane	elephant	police car
4	bicycle	car	balloon	truck

🔊⁴⁸ Listen again.

D4

It's the blue truck.

Play a game: Three guesses.

Is it in A4?

Is it in D4?

The blue truck. You have three guesses.

No, it isn't.

Yes, it is!

Unit 10

♪ The Song of the Spider

Sing.

I have long, black legs,
I have a big, hairy nose,
I have six yellow eyes,
And eight hairy toes.

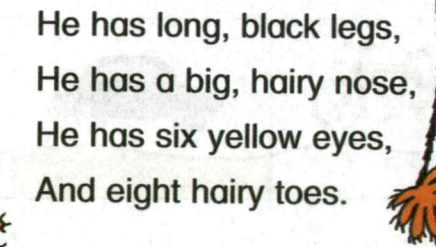

I'm Sam the Spider!
Ho! Ho! Ho!
I'm Sam the Spider!
Ha! Ha! Ha!
I'm Sam the Spider!
Sam the Spider.
Sam the Spider.
Hey! Hey! Hey!

He has long, black legs,
He has a big, hairy nose,
He has six yellow eyes,
And eight hairy toes.

He's Sam the Spider!
Ho! Ho! Ho!
He's Sam the Spider!
Ha! Ha! Ha!
He's Sam the Spider!
Sam the Spider.
Sam the Spider.
Hey! Hey! Hey!

Unit 11

Do you have a TV?

🎧⁵⁰ **Listen.**

Answer: ☑ *Yes, I do.* or ☒ *No, I don't.*

"Do you have a TV, Lucy?"
"Do you have a computer?"
"Yes, I do."
"No, I don't."

a TV ✓	a computer	a cat	a dog
a car	a radio	a ball	a swimming pool

Now ask your friend: *Do you have…?*

Play a game: Hide the crayon.

"Do you have my green crayon?"
"No, I don't."
"Do you have my blue crayon?"
"Yes, I do."

Unit 11

The telephone number

Unit 11

43

Elephants? Tigers? Acrobats?

🔊52 Look and listen.

Answer: *Yes, it does.* or *No, it doesn't.*

COME TO THE RED, WHITE, AND BLUE CIRCUS TODAY!

See the lions and the elephants, the acrobats and the clowns, the horses and Mr. Muscles, the strongest man in the world!

Does the circus have horses?

Yes, it does.

Does it have tigers?

No, it doesn't.

Play a game: Find the name.

1. Think of a name.

ANTONIA

2. A boy or a girl?

Is it a boy or a girl?

A girl.

3. Find the name.

Does she have an "A" in her name?

Yes, she does.

Unit 11

🎵 Cats, Hats, and Acrobats

Sing.

We have big, black cats,
We have dancing dogs,
We have yellow, paper hats...

We have small, brown clowns,
We have a big strongman,
We have happy acrobats...

At the circus,
Yes, we do...
At the circus,
Just for you!

At the circus,
Yes, we do...
At the circus,
Just for you!

Listen and repeat.

white cat   black cat   white cat   black cat   white cat   black cat   white cat

Unit 12

45

The STOP! GO! coin game

🔊 55 **Listen and repeat.**

a square   a triangle   a circle   a rectangle

Read and play the game.

THE STOP! GO! COIN GAME

START HERE

STOP! Wait here.
GO! Go to the blue rectangle.

STOP! Wait here.
GO! Go to the yellow circle.

STOP! Wait here.
GO! Go to the orange triangle.

STOP! Wait here.
GO! Go to the green triangle.

STOP! Wait here.
GO! Go to the red square.

STOP! Wait here.
GO! Go to the white circle.

You're here! Very good!

Unit 12

📼 The yellow circles

1.
- Follow the yellow circles, Lucy. OK? Please find me.
- Yes, yellow circles, with a crayon.
- The yellow circles?

2.
- I'm in a big truck with my family.

3.
- Look, Bicycle! A yellow circle.
- And here's a yellow circle, too.

4.
- Look! A yellow circle again. Come on!
- Listen! It's a telephone.

Unit 12

Is it sweet?

🔊⁵⁷ Look, listen, and answer.

a. a tree
b. a car
c. a building
d. a building
e. a tree
f. a car

Play a game: Is it sweet? Is it sour? Is it salty?

Is it sweet? — No, it isn't. It's...

Is it sour? — Yes, it is.

Is it salty? — No, it isn't. It's...

Unit 12

🎵 The Drawing Song

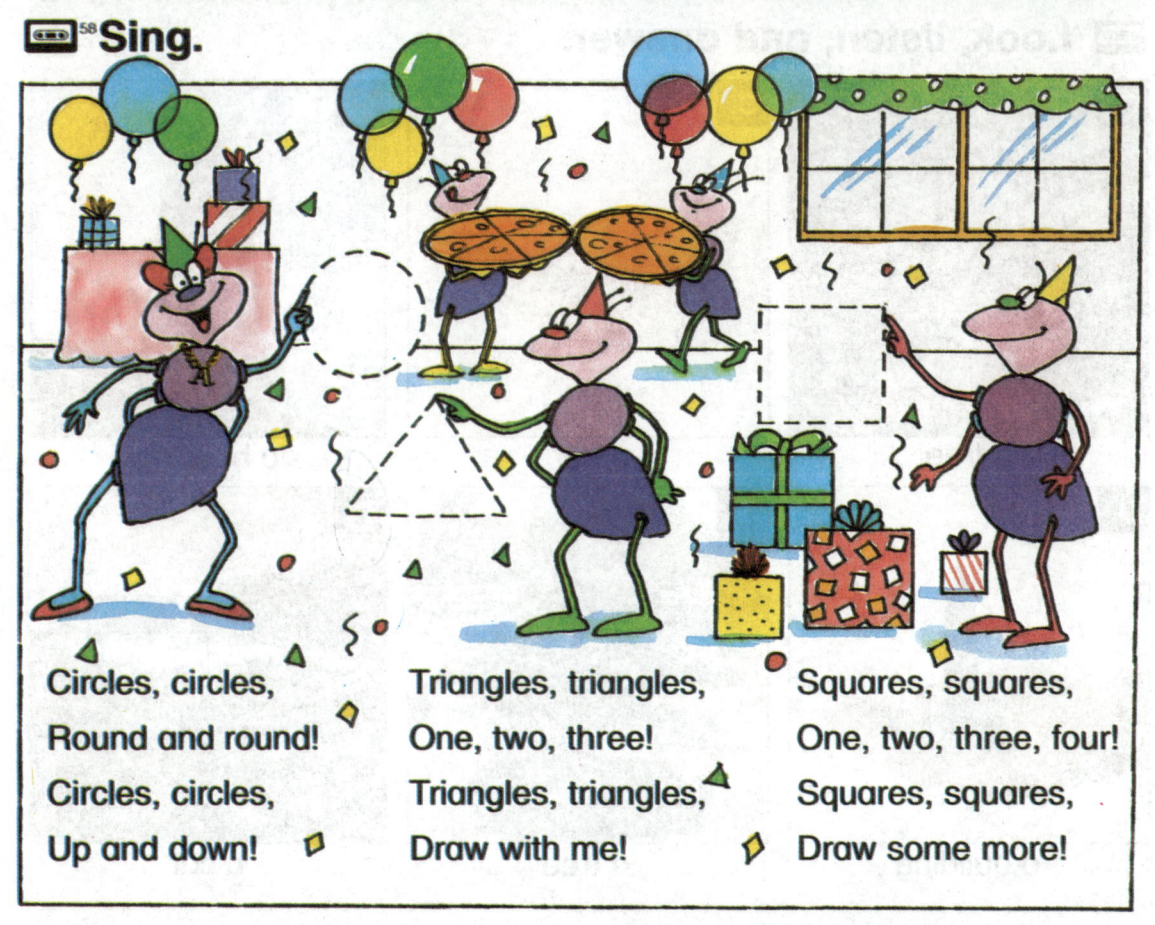

Sing.

Circles, circles,
Round and round!
Circles, circles,
Up and down!

Triangles, triangles,
One, two, three!
Triangles, triangles,
Draw with me!

Squares, squares,
One, two, three, four!
Squares, squares,
Draw some more!

Play a game: Squares, triangles, and circles.

1. Look at the picture.

Find two... circles!

Quick! Find a circle!

2. Listen to your teacher.

Stop! Here are two circles!

Find one... square!

Unit 13

49

Ants in his pants

🎧⁵⁹ Listen, read, and match.

There's a monster in my bag!

There are ants in my pants!

There's a spider in my pocket!

There's an insect in my ear!

Help! There are snakes in my shoes!

Play a game: Who am I?

Listen. Who am I?

There are ants in my pants!

You're Herman!

Unit 13

The red, white, and blue truck

1. Hi. It's Montgomery again. Do you have Zoko and the bicycle with you?

Yes, we do. They're here.

2. Good! Does the bicycle have a bell?

Yes, it does.

Good! Ring the bell again and again. Then stop and listen.

OK!

3. There are five or six trucks over there.

There's a red, white, and blue circus truck!

Ring the bell again, Zoko! Now listen!

4. Help! We're in here!

They're in the red, white, and blue truck.

Quick, open the door!

Unit 13

Is there a teacher in the classroom?

🎧⁶¹ **Listen and look at this classroom.**

Answer: *Yes, there is.* or *No, there isn't.*

Is there a cat in the classroom?

🎧⁶² **Listen again.**

Now answer: *Yes, there are.* or *No, there aren't.*

Are there any girls in the classroom?

Now ask your friends about *your* classroom.

Are there any bags?

Is there a computer?

52 Unit 13

🎵 No School!

🔊 ⁶³ Sing.

There's a lemonade river.
There's a chocolate bus.
There's an ice cream cone for you all.
There's a candy store.
There's a hot dog stand.
And there isn't any school!
No, there isn't any school!

There are red balloons.
There are bubbles and balls.
There are bells.
There are songs.
There are acrobats.
There are clowns in hats.
And there isn't any school!
No, there isn't any school!

Unit 14

53

Zoko, the hot dog, and the french fries

Look and read.

There's an ant *in* the box.

Help!

Now the ant is *near* the box.

Now the ant is *on* the box.

🔊⁶⁴ **Listen and point.**

🔊⁶⁵ **Listen again. You are Zoko. Answer:** *Yes* or *No.*

Read. Answer: ✓ *Right* or ✗ *Wrong.*

☐ 1. The apples are near the popcorn box.

☐ 2. The popcorn box is near the french fries.

☐ 3. The ice cream is near the candy box.

Unit 14

Where are the clowns?

1. It's OK. I have very strong hands. / Come on, Montgomery! Quick! Hide! / Very good, Zoko!

2. It's Mr. Stink and his friend. / The door is open! Where is Montgomery? / Where are the clowns?

3. Ready? / NOW! / POP! / POP!

4. Help! Quick! It's the police! Run! Hide in the truck! / BANG! / Hello? Police? This is Montgomery the Clown....

Unit 14

55

Find the ghosts.

67 Listen and look.
Answer: *Yes, there is.* or *Yes, there are.*

68 Listen again.
Answer: *It's in/near...* or *They're in/near... .*

69 Listen and repeat.

gray ghost   green ghost   gray ghost   green ghost   gray ghost   green ghost

Unit 14

🎵 Where Are You Now?

Sing.

Where's the blue sky?
Where's the sun?
Where's the music?
Where's the song?

Who is with you now, my friend?
Where are you now?
Where are you now?

Where are the birds?
Where are the trees?
Where are the flowers?
Where are the bees?

Who is with you now, my friend?
Where are you now?
Where are you now?

Unit 15

57

Look again, please. (*Review*)

a b c

Look again at page 4.

🔊⁷¹ Sing the song.

Look again at page 13.

Play the game: How do you spell…?

How do you spell *her* name?

How do you spell *his* name?

Numbers and colors

Look again at page 21.

Count the balloons.

Look again at page 33.

🔊⁷³ Listen and repeat with Zoko.

🔊⁷⁴ Listen and point.

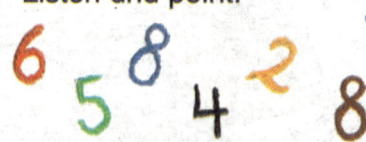

6 8 2 4
5 4 8

🔊⁷⁵ Sing the song on page 24 again.

What's this?

Look and answer. What's this?

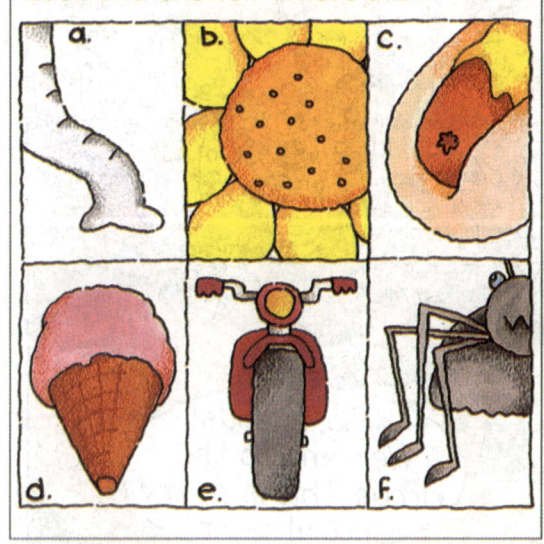

a. b. c.
d. e. f.

Who's this?

Look again at page 11.

Who are they?

Look again at page 12.

🔊⁷² Sing the song.

Read, ask, and answer.

Ask your friends:
1. What's your name?
2. How do you spell your name?
3. How old are you?
4. What color are your eyes?
5. What is the name of your English book?
6. What color is it?

🔊⁷⁶ Sing the song on page 36 again.

Unit 15

A very special night

1. The next night.

Hello, friends! Welcome to the circus! This is a very special night.

2. I have five special friends with me.

My friends are... Lucy, ...Herman and Shep, ...Annie, ...and Zoko, the clever robot!

I'm clever!

3. And tonight, friends, we have Simba the Lion, and there are the elephants from India. And...

Ready?

Yes! NOW!

OH, NO! STOP!

4. OK, clowns. Where are you?

Run! Quick!

GREAT!

Unit 15

Look again, please. (*Review*)

Big or small?

Look again at page 31.

Play the game: What's this?

Look again at page 32.

🔊⁷⁸ Sing the song.

Faces, arms, and legs

Look again at page 37.

Play the game: Who's this?

Look again at page 40.

🔊⁷⁹ Sing the song.

Circles and squares

Look again at page 45.

Play the STOP! GO! coin game again.

Close your books

Draw the picture of the circle, triangle, rectangle, and square again.

Where's the orange triangle?...the blue rectangle?...the yellow circle?...the red square?

Look again at page 48.

🔊⁸⁰ Sing the song and play the game on that page.

There is.../There are...

Look again at page 49.

Read and match again.

Look again at the picture on page 51.

Ask your friends questions: *Is there...? Are there...?* Look again at page 52.

🔊⁸¹ Sing the song.

In, on, or near?

Look again at page 53.

Now ask your friends, *Where is...*

the teacher? your English book?
my notebook? your school bag?
the Empire State Building?

Look again at page 56.

🔊⁸² Sing the song.

Read, ask, and answer

Ask your friends:
1. Do you have a computer?
2. Do you have a cat or a dog?
3. Do you have a radio?
4. Do you have a telephone?
5. Do you have a big nose?
6. Do you have three eyes?
7. Do you have hairy hands?
8. Do you have green ears?

Look again at page 43.

Play the game: Find the name.

Unit 15

🎵 It's Time To Say Goodbye!

Sing.

It's time, it's time
For a holiday.
It's time to say goodbye!

It's time to sing, and
It's time to dance.
It's time to say goodbye!

It's time, it's time
For a great party.
It's time to say goodbye!

It's time for music, and
It's time for a song.
It's time to say goodbye!

Scope and Sequence Chart

Unit		Language items
1	page 1	The alphabet: small letters
		Classroom commands (1)
2	page 5	Greetings; *I'm...; Goodbye.*
		Classroom commands (2)
		Identifying things: *What's this?* (1); *a* + noun
3	page 9	*What's this?* (2); *a* + noun (continued)
		Introductions (1): *Who's this? This is...*
		Requests: *Give me a..., please. Thank you.*
4	page 13	The alphabet: capital letters
		Introductions (2): *This is my (brother/sister).*
		My and *your*: *What's your name? My name's...*
5	page 17	*What's this? It's a...*
		an + nouns with initial vowel *(a, e, i, o, u)*
		Language Review
6	page 21	Numbers 1–10
		How old are you?
		Be: I'm.../We're...
7	page 25	*How old is he/she?*
		Be continued: *He's.../She's.../They're...*
		Possessions: *his/her*
8	page 29	*Is it a/an...?*
		Yes, it is./No, it isn't.
		Adjectives (1): *It's a big/small* + noun

Scope and Sequence Chart continued

Unit	Language items
9 page 33	Saying where you are from: *I'm from.../He's from...* *The* + noun Adjectives (2): colors
10 page 37	Describing appearance: *I have* + parts of face/head *She/he has* + regular plural nouns *(ears, arms, legs)* Adjectives (3): *tall, short, long, thin* Language Review
11 page 41	*Do you have a/my/your/the...?* *Yes, I do./No, I don't.* *Does he/she have...?* *Yes/No...*
12 page 45	Shapes *Is it* (+ adjective)?
13 page 49	Describing places: *There's.../There are...* *Is there...?/Are there...?* *Yes/No...*
14 page 53	Talking about location: *Where's the...?/Where are the...?* Prepositions of place: *in, on, near*
15 page 57	Language Review